The *Substitute Survival Kit* was designed to take the "guess-work" out of subbing. Every successful substitute teacher plans ahead to provide a positive learning experience for students. By following the steps below, and utilizing all parts of this book, the more organized you will be and the smoother your day will go.

A. Keep accurate records of where you've taught, dates, grade levels, etc. Using the **Calendar and Assignment Records** on page 2 will help you accomplish this. Make several copies of this page to keep on file. Most schools will let you use their copier for school business such as this.

B. Always take a **tote bag** along with you, filled with everything you will need. Don't count on the school to have supplies. Contents for your bag might be . . .

IF Substitute Survival Kit	transparent tape	ruler
coffee cup	pencils	scissors
tissues	paper – graph and plain	puppets
stapler	paper clips	flash cards (p. 6)
markers	pens	cookie cutters (p. 7)
construction paper	glue stick	Nerf™ ball (p. 6)

children's books to read aloud (pages 10-13) –
   Miss Nelson Is Missing/Miss Nelson Is Back by Harry Allard
   Alexander and the Terrible, Horrible, No Good, Very Bad Day by Judith Viorst
   The Day Jimmy's Boa Ate the Wash by Trinka Hakes Noble
   Where the Sidewalk Ends by Shel Silverstein

tapes –
   Free To Be You and Me, and *Peter, Paul and Mommy* (both contain some of Shel Silverstein's poems)

C. **Dress appropriately**. You may be going outside, sitting on the floor, or working on an art project.

D. Keep a supply of **awards** and **patterns** (pages 4-5) on hand. Also, check out the easy **art** and **science** suggestions (pages 20-21) ahead of time in case you would like to collect materials to take along for an experiment and/or an art activity.

E. Arrive at school in plenty of time to familiarize yourself with the school, lesson plans, and schedule. If lesson plans were left for you, try your best to stick to them so the class will stay on schedule. If not, you will need to write lesson plans of your own and make copies of our activity pages before school begins.

F. At the end of the day fill out a copy of the **Substitute Class Report** (page 3) for the classroom teacher. The information on that report will help give the teacher a good idea of how the day went and which lessons you were able to cover. You may want to keep a copy for your files.

 # Record/Calendar

Assignment Record

Date: _____ A.M. ____ P.M. ____

District: _____

School: _____

Teacher: _____ Grade: _____

Time School Begins/Ends: _____

Comments on Assignment: _____

_____

Directions to School: _____

_____

_____

Date Paid: _____

Assignment Record

Date: _____ A.M. ____ P.M. ____

District: _____

School: _____

Teacher: _____ Grade: _____

Time School Begins/Ends: _____

Comments on Assignment: _____

_____

Directions to School: _____

_____

_____

Date Paid: _____

Month of _____

 # Class Report

Substitute Teacher _____ Date _____

School _____ Classroom Teacher _____ Grade _____

Students absent: _____

The following students . . .

☐ were especially helpful – _____

_____

☐ exhibited disruptive behavior – _____

_____

☐ Comments: _____

_____

The class . . .

☐ followed classroom rules.   ☐ worked hard on assignments.

☐ was courteous and helpful.   ☐ _____

The lesson plans . . .

☐ were completed.   ☐ were not completed.

The subjects/assignments not completed were . . .

1. _____

2. _____

3. _____

Other _____

Comments: _____

_____

_____

My experience as a substitute was . . .

☐ satisfactory/positive.   ☐ less than satisfactory.

Comments: _____

_____

You can assist your substitute in having a good day by . . . _____

_____

 # Class Awards

This Award Is Given To:

_____

For: _____

_____ _____
Teacher   Date

This Award Has Been Given To:

_____

for: _____

_____ _____
Teacher   Date

Name

Name

Name

 IF450 Substitute Survival Kit

Do You Remember?

Materials – twelve to fifteen items ordinarily found in a classroom, for example: marker, paper, eraser, pencil, ruler, chalk, book, etc.

Procedure:

• Show the class each of the objects, one by one.

• Have the students close their eyes. Remove the objects from view.

• Direct the students to open their eyes and write down as many objects as they can remember on their papers.

Dog and Bone

Materials – chalkboard eraser or ruler

Procedure:

• Choose a student to be the "dog."

• Have the dog sit in a chair at the front of the classroom, facing away from the class.

• Place the "bone" (eraser or ruler) on the floor behind the dog.

• Tap a student from the class. This student is to steal the bone quietly from behind the dog.

• The dog barks if he or she hears the bone being stolen.

• The student who can steal the bone without being detected becomes the new dog.

Variations – Witch and Broom, Pilgrim and Turkey, Santa and Toy, Easter Bunny and Egg

Let's Change

Procedure:

• Students number off from one to the number of students in the class. Choose one student to be the caller.

• Have the students stand in a circle, with the caller in the center. Students in the circle should not be in numerical order.

• The caller calls two numbers. The players whose numbers are called must run to switch places. The caller attemtpts to take one of the emptied spaces.

• The player who is left without a place becomes the next caller, and the game continues.

Hoppin'

Materials – flash cards

Procedure:

• Show and read aloud selected flash cards of addition or subtraction facts.

• Give each student a chance to "hop" the answers to one or two flash cards. For example, for a flash card that has 2 + 3, the student would hop five times.

• If the student hops correctly, he or she may flash the next card to the next student.

• Rotate until everyone has had at least one chance to hop an answer.

Numbers Up!

Materials – large rubber playground ball

Procedure:

• Have students form a circle and number off from one to the number of students in the class. Choose one student to be the caller. The caller stands in the center of the circle and holds the ball.

• The caller tosses the ball high into the air and calls one number. The student whose number is called must try to catch the ball before it bounces more than once. If successful, the catcher becomes the next caller.

• If the catcher does not get the ball before the second bounce, the caller may have another turn at calling out a different number and playing another round.

Silence, Please!

Materials – small rubber ball or Nerf™ Ball

Procedure:

• Have students sit on their desktops, without having their feet touch the floor.

• The students must pass the ball from one to another without talking or dropping the ball.

• Any student who talks, drops the ball, or makes a careless pass causing the receiving student to drop the ball is out and must be seated on a chair.

• The game continues until one student remains. That student is the winner.

Draw a Face

Materials – large faces from magazines, colored pencils or crayons, manila paper (one sheet per student), pencils, glue

Directions:

- Fold and cut in half faces gathered from magazines.

- Distribute half faces to students.

- Glue the half face on the manila paper.

- With a pencil, lightly sketch the missing half of the face: hair, neck, etc.

- Color the drawing to match the picture from the magazine.

Puffy Clouds

Materials – sheets of blue construction paper, cotton balls, glue

Directions:

- Take the students outside to look at the clouds or just look out a window. Encourage them to look for the shape of an animal or an object in the clouds. Have the students duplicate what they saw using cotton balls.

- Demonstrate how cotton balls can be pulled apart to cover a larger space and/or make a desired shape. They are to glue the cotton balls to the construction paper.

Cookie Cutter Creations

Materials – one sheet of drawing paper per student, several cookie cutters to share, pencils, crayons

Directions:

- Have each student think about the picture he/she is going to draw. Then have them trace the cookie-cutter shape(s) where they want it in their picture.

- Draw and color in the features or details needed to complete the picture created by the outline of the cookie cutter.

- Draw and color a background scene.

Giant Jigsaw Puzzles

Materials – tagboard, black marker, crayons

Directions:

- Divide the class into groups of 4.

- Give each group a large piece of tagboard on which "jigsaw" puzzle lines have been drawn with a black marker. Be sure the lines are in different patterns on each tagboard. The number of pieces will depend on the age and ability level of the students.

- Each group is to design and color a picture on the puzzle.

- When finished, they are to cut the puzzle apart along the marker lines and exchange their puzzle with another group. Keep the pieces in a large envelope or folder.

Shape Art

Materials – drawing paper, pencil, crayons

Directions:

- Use only shapes such as triangles, circles, and/or squares for the drawing.

- Draw a picture of an animal or object, using various sizes of the shapes.

- Color the drawing.

Enlarging Pictures

Materials – copies of graph on page 9, pictures shown here, pencils

Directions:

- Reproduce two graph pages per student and pictures below.

- Demonstrate how to enlarge a picture using graph paper. Point out that students need to carefully copy one square at a time on their graph paper.

- Use one of the sheets of graph paper to enlarge the picture of the house.

- Repeat the procedure with the dinosaur on the second sheet of graph paper.

Use for Enlarging Pictures, page 8.

Literature

Alexander and the Terrible, Horrible, No Good, Very Bad Day
by Judith Viorst

Everyone certainly has days when nothing seems to go right, Alexander has one of those days. Your students will fill the classroom with chuckles as they relive Alexander's day with him. This book is a comical catalyst for a follow-up discussion on how to handle those days when nothing turns out as planned.

8:00	10:00	12:00	2:00	4:00	6:00	8:00
ouT for breakfast	Field Trip	🥪	Recess	cAndy STore	EaT dinner	📖

What If?

What if Alexander woke up the next morning and found a lucky penny under his pillow and proceeded to have the most wonderful day of his life? First make a chart on the blackboard listing key times of the day, such as 8:00, 10:00, 12:00, 2:00, 4:00, 6:00 and 8:00. Decide together what Alexander might be doing at each of these times. The students then write about and/or draw what happened in each time frame.

Miss Nelson Is Missing!/Miss Nelson Is Back
by Harry Allard

Miss Nelson Is Missing! and its sequel Miss Nelson Is Back are wonderfully insightful promotions of teacher appreciation. After the terror of Miss Viola Swamp, the students in these stories realize that their own teacher, Miss Nelson, is truly a wonderful teacher!

Show Stoppers

Pass out Popsicle sticks and construction paper scraps to your students to make stick puppets of the characters in both of the Miss Nelson books. Then have the students retell the stories in their own words, using the puppets.

Miss Nelson Says

Adapt the game of "Simon Says" to this book by choosing a Miss Nelson (Simon) to begin the game. Substitute the phrase "Miss Nelson Says" for "Simon Says."

The Day Jimmy's Boa Ate the Wash
by Trinka Hakes Noble

A class trip to a farm is usually not as exciting and adventurous as the one Jimmy's class from the 12th Street School experienced. The elaborate answers to the question "How was the class trip to the farm?" asked by one of the student's mothers, will definitely catch your class's attention.

Brown Bag Barnyard Puppets

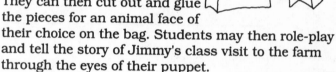

Make puppets of barnyard animals out of brown lunch bags and construction paper. Draw a few simple examples of faces of barnyard animals on the blackboard. You may also use patterns if you feel the students need more direction. They can then cut out and glue the pieces for an animal face of their choice on the bag. Students may then role-play and tell the story of Jimmy's class visit to the farm through the eyes of their puppet.

Where the Sidewalk Ends
by Shel Silverstein

"If you are a dreamer, come in . . . " to the world where the sidewalk ends and the magical poems of Shel Silverstein begin.
Illustrated by . . .

The poems listed below evoke vivid images. Try reading these to the class without showing them Shel Silverstein's illustrations. Children can then illustrate what they envision as they listen. Share drawings with one another. When you are finished, show the class the book illustrations to show what the author envisioned as he wrote each poem.

Poems:
"Sick"   "Eighteen Flavors"
"Merry . . . "   "Sarah Cynthia Sylvia Stout"
"Band-Aids"
"Recipe for a Hippopotamus Sandwich"

What a Day!

Read the poem "What a Day," then write it on the chalkboard, omitting lines 3, 4, 5 and 6. Have the students copy the lines from the board, then create their own lines 3-6 describing one of their worst days. Let students illustrate this never-to-be-forgotten day. Then write the author's original lines on the chalkboard for the children to compare.

Alexander and the Terrible, Horrible, No Good,
Very Bad Day

The Horrible, No Good, Very Bad Day

Name _____

A	B	C	D	E	F	G	H	I	J	K	L	M
1	2	3	4	5	6	7	8	9	10	11	12	13

N	O	P	Q	R	S	T	U	V	W	X	Y	Z
14	15	16	17	18	19	20	21	22	23	24	25	26

Use the number code to find the missing words.

1. Alexander tripped over his _____.
   19-11-1-20-5-2-15-1-18-4

2. Then he dropped his _____ in the sink.
   19-23-5-1-20-5-18

3. Alexander never found a _____ in his cereal box.
   16-18-9-26-5

4. On the way to school, he did not get a seat by the
   _____.
   23-9-14-4-15-23

5. His teacher did not like his drawing of an _____
   _____.
   9-14-22-9-19-9-2-12-5
   3-1-19-20-12-5

6. His mom forgot to pack _____ in his lunchbox.
   4-5-19-19-5-18-20

7. Alexander forgot the number _____ when
   counting.
   19-9-24-20-5-5-14

8. Alexander was the only one who had a _____ at
   the dentist's office.
   3-1-22-9-20-25

9. At the _____, he got plain white sneakers.
   19-8-15-5   19-20-15-18-5

10. If things didn't get better soon, Alexander was going to move
    to _____.
    1-21-19-20-18-1-12-9-1

Do You Know a Boa?

Name _____

Print a rhyming word under each word on the boa's body. Slither down from the head to the tail. Ssssssssssssss.

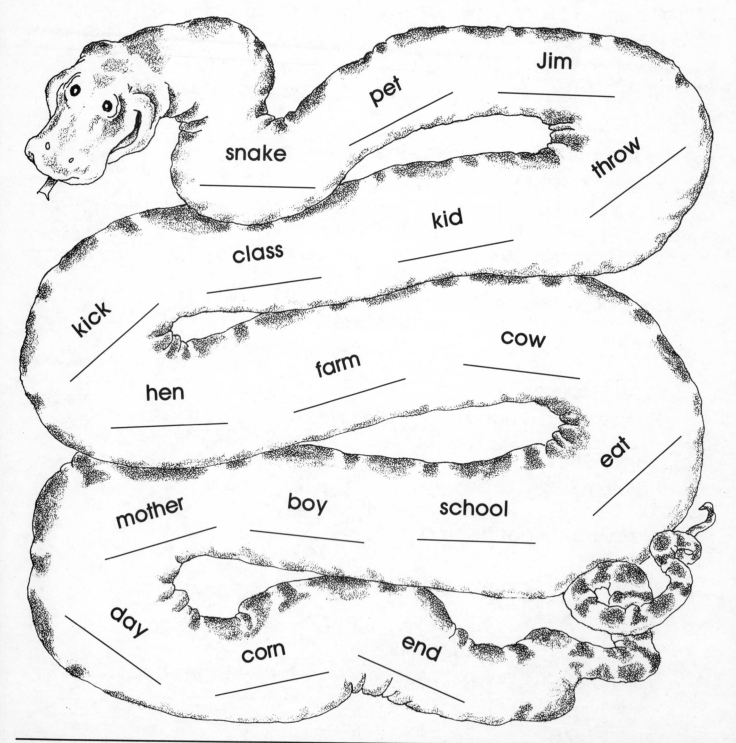

Miss Nelson Is Missing!/Miss Nelson Is Back

Desk Jockeys

Name _____

Put the words from Miss Nelson's desk under the characters they best describe. Then draw the characters in the boxes below the word lists.

Miss Nelson	Mr. Blandsworth	Viola Swamp
_____	_____	_____
_____	_____	_____
_____	_____	_____
_____	_____	_____
_____	_____	_____

blonde	sweet
boring	substitute
ill	loud
soft-spoken	mean
man	mustache
confused	funny tie
principal	kind
black fingernails	sore throat
strict	black dress

Farm Shapes

Name _____

Color:

brown   yellow   green   red

Subtraction Hill

Name _____

Work all problems to find path. Shade in all
answers that have a 3 in them.

		98 − 52	46 − 12	68 − 17
	79 − 53	65 − 23	63 − 31	86 − 32
59 − 45	75 − 64	67 − 24	97 − 54	55 − 43

87 − 65	44 − 32	57 − 24	88 − 25	75 − 61	48 − 26
69 − 25	95 − 24	48 − 13	58 − 16	35 − 13	39 − 17

Shape Mates

Match the congruent figures.

Name _____

1. 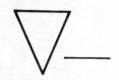 ____

2. ____ ____

3. ____

4. ____

5. ____

6. ____

7. ____

8.  ____

9. ____

10. ____

11. ____

12. ____

13. ____

14. ____

15. ____

16. ____

17. ____

18. ____

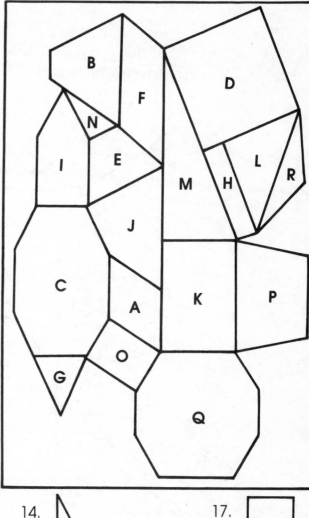

B
F
D
N
I
E
L
R
M
H
J
C
K
P
A
O
G
Q

IF450 Substitute Survival Kit

Minute Maid

Name _____

How long does it take the "Minute Maid" to do her household tasks?

	Time Started	Length of Task	Time Ended
Polishing	Example 9:14	35 minutes	9:49
Dusting		42 minutes	8:00
Waxing	10:03		10:51
Mopping	2:36	29 minutes	
Cleaning Windows	4:45		5:32
Serving Breakfast		18 minutes	7:30
Laundry	11:10	58 minutes	
Ironing	12:13		1:00
Serving Lunch	11:30	24 minutes	
Vacuuming		41 minutes	3:57
Serving Dinner	5:30		5:57
Hanging Curtains	6:26	56 minutes	
Making Beds	8:03		8:41

Math

One-Stop Shopping

Name _____

Stash McCash is shopping! Find the total cost of the items. Then find how much change Stash should receive.

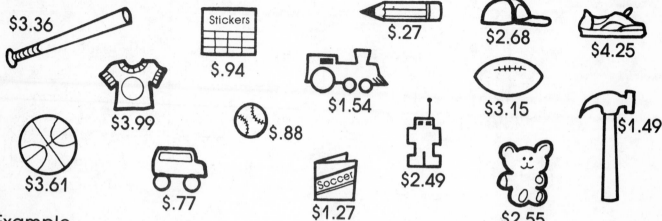

$3.36 Stickers $.94 $.27 $2.68 $4.25
$3.99 $1.54 $3.15 $1.49
$.88 $2.49
$3.61 $.77 Soccer $1.27 $2.55

Example

Stash has $5.00	Stash has $8.50	Stash has $7.04	Stash has $9.00

Example (column 1):
Stash has $5.00
Buys

.88
.77
+1.54
3.19

5.00
−3.19
1.81 Change

Column 2: Stash has $8.50 Buys — Change

Column 3: Stash has $7.04 Buys — Change

Column 4: Stash has $9.00 Buys — Change

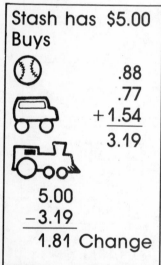  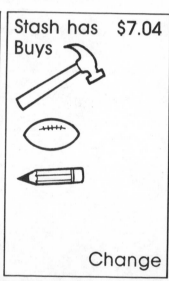 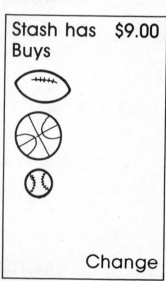

Stash has $10.95 Buys — Change
Stash has $10.00 Buys — Change
Stash has $9.24 Buys — Change
Stash has $8.09 Buys — Change

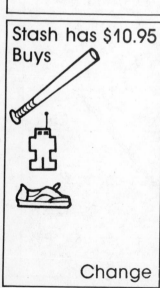   

©1993 Instructional Fair, Inc.

18

IF450 Substitute Survival Kit

Step Right Up

Name _____

Start at the bottom of the steps. Write your answer at the top.

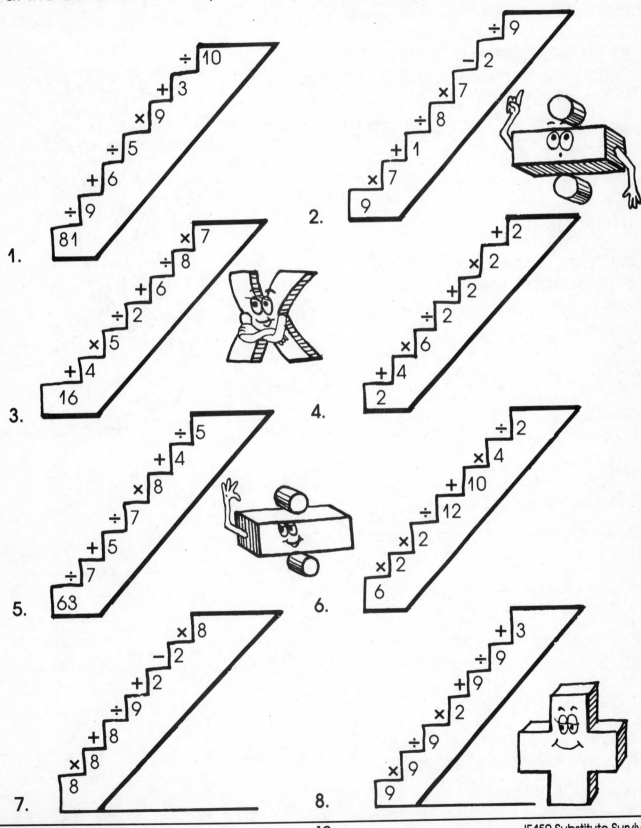

1.
```
÷ 10
+ 3
× 9
÷ 5
+ 6
÷ 9
81
```

2.
```
÷ 9
− 2
× 7
÷ 8
+ 1
× 7
9
```

3.
```
× 7
÷ 8
+ 6
÷ 2
× 5
+ 4
16
```

4.
```
+ 2
× 2
+ 2
÷ 2
× 6
+ 4
2
```

5.
```
÷ 5
+ 4
× 8
÷ 7
+ 5
÷ 7
63
```

6.
```
÷ 2
× 4
+ 10
÷ 12
× 2
× 2
6
```

7.
```
× 8
− 2
+ 2
÷ 9
+ 8
× 8
8
```

8.
```
+ 3
÷ 9
+ 9
× 2
÷ 9
× 9
9
```

Bag It!

Name _____

Do

Put 10 small objects in a plastic bag.
Close the bag with a rubber band.
Put the bag into a lunch sack.
Close the lunch sack with a rubber band.

Trading Sacks

Exchange sacks with a friend.
Do not open the sack.
Feel the sack carefully for a few minutes.

List

List what you think you felt in the sack.
Guess at the ones you do not know.

1. _____
2. _____
3. _____
4. _____
5. _____

6. _____
7. _____
8. _____
9. _____
10. _____

Opening the Sack

How many did you get right? _____
Which object was the biggest surprise? _____

Science

Shape Up

Name _____

FACTS FOR THIS LESSON

There are certain shapes that you can find in many ordinary natural things. Looking for these shapes will help you to sharpen your powers of observation. The first column on the right has 5 of these basic shapes.

Practice looking for the shapes by drawing a line from each tree in the second column to its basic shape.

WHAT TO DO

Go outdoors, and look all around you for the shapes listed below. Two new shapes have been added: spiral 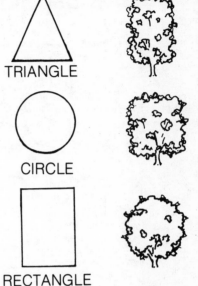 and radial 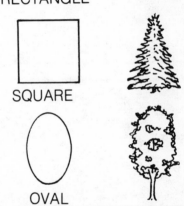 . Try to find two or three examples of each shape. You may have to look very carefully to find some of them. Find examples in animals as well as plants.

Fill in the chart as you find examples of each shape. One has been started for you.

SHAPE	NATURAL OBJECT
triangle	
rectangle	
square	
circle	
oval	
spiral	*snail*
radial	

The triangle, circle, rectangle, square, and oval shapes appear with trees matched to basic shapes.

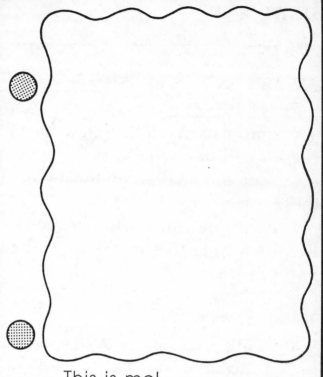

Name _____

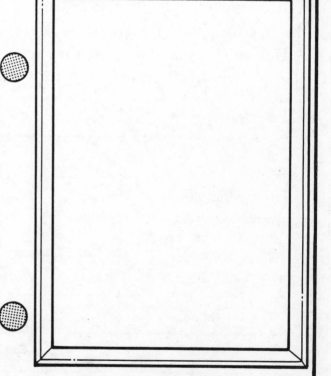

This is me!
I am _____ years old.

This is where I live.

This is my family.

Map It Out

Name _____

Use the legend box to answer the questions.

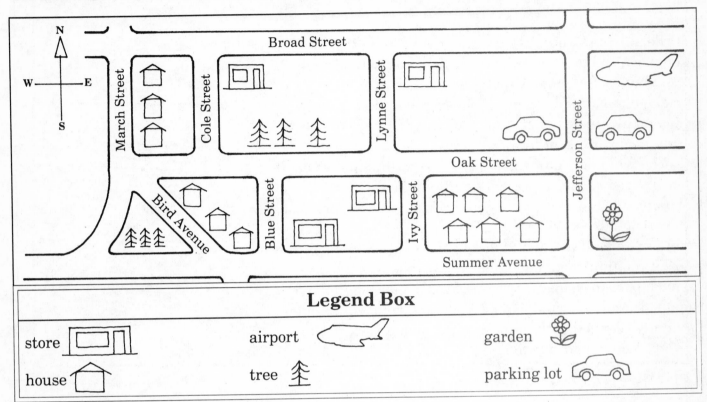

1. Does Star City have an airport? _____
2. How many houses are on Bird Avenue? _____
3. What is on the corner of Oak Street and Jefferson Street? _____
4. The garden is on the corner of Jefferson Street and _____.
5. How many stores are in Star City? _____
6. What direction is Summer Avenue from Oak Street? _____
7. Which street is directly west of Ivy Street? _____
8. How many trees are north of Oak Street? _____
9. How many houses are between Ivy Street and Jefferson Street? _____
10. How many stores are north of Summer Avenue? _____
11. How many parking lots are east of Lynne Street? _____
12. What street is south of the garden? _____
13. What two items are found in the block between Lynne Street and Jefferson Street? _____
14. How many houses are there in all on this map? _____

Design a Community

Use with page 25.

Name _____

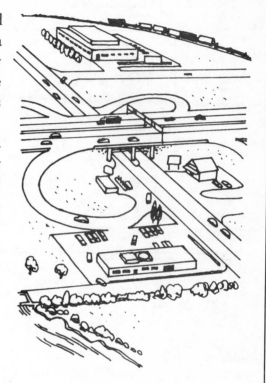

People influence the environment when they build human communities. In this lesson you will design a community for about 10,000 people. You will do this by making a map of land use. Your map will only show the community in a very general way. It will not show streets or schools or vacant lots.

You will plan your community by coloring squares on a map. Each square represents a city block. You will color less than half of the squares on the map. The squares that you do not color will remain farmland. (Try not to leave a lot of farmland in the middle of your community.)

As you think about and plan your community, you may need to make changes. You should first make your plan in pencil. Add color only when you have your entire community planned. Try to make the community a place in which you would like to live.

DO THIS

1. Think of a name for your community. Write the name at the top of the map.
2. Color the lake and the stream blue.
3. Select 25 squares for shopping areas. Shopping areas should be near major roads. Place some shopping squares in a central area for a shopping center. Also place some shopping squares near the Interstate exit for restaurants and gas stations. Lightly mark a small "s" inside the shopping areas so that you will remember what they are.
4. Select 50 squares for factories. Some factories are small, some are very large. Factories need to be next to railroads and highways so that they can ship their products. Also, factories create a great deal of noise and smoke so they should be away from houses. Lightly mark an "f" inside the factory areas.
5. Select about 100 squares for parks. Place some park area along the river for walking and biking. Save some park squares so that you can place them among the housing. The number of squares for parks may not be exact, because along the river you will be dealing with only parts of squares. Lightly mark them "p."
6. Select 350 squares for housing. Lightly mark them "h."
7. After you are satisfied with your community plan, color shopping squares red, factory squares purple, park squares green, and housing squares yellow.

Design a Community

Name _____

A PLAN FOR _____

(name of the community)

LAKE

RIVER

SWAMP

Key:
═══ Interstate
─── Major road
+++ Railroad

Scale of miles
0   ½   1

Creative Writing

Lost and Found

Name _____

Add the missing parts to the story. Complete the sign describing the lost article.

One beautiful, sunshiny day _____ was on the way home from school

with_____ friend _____ . They cut through the park

and _____ .

While they were there _____ .

Later _____

_____ . _____

decided _____ .

It read:

> ## Found:_____
>
> Loser may claim it by
> _____
> _____

After _____ got home, _____

_____

_____ .

The next day _____ saw a sign on the_____

_____

_____ .

"I was_____," _____told _____ friend.

" _____

_____

_____

Just like any other night, you crawl into bed and fall fast asleep. The next morning you wake up to find that it is either a hundred years in the future or in the past. Write about your experiences and tell how you would get back to your own time.

In the middle of the night, a noise outside your bedroom window woke you up. Describe what the noise sounded like. Tell what or who made the noise, etc.

One day, while in the library, you take a book off the shelf. As you are about to put it back, you notice a key taped to the back of the shelf with a note attached to it. What does the note say? What do you do with the key? Where does the key lead you?

A new student comes to your class. What can you tell him that will help him learn about your school, your teacher, and your classroom? What will you do to make him feel welcome?

Your father bought an old desk at an auction. After he brought it home, you found an old hand-drawn map in the back of one small drawer. Draw the map and explain what you think it means.

A terrible storm comes to your city and you cannot go anywhere for three days. Tell about the storm, and what you will do during those three days.

Oh no! It's spring cleaning time again. Everyone helps – no escaping this task! Your job is to clean out the basement. You go downstairs and find box upon box and stack upon stack of junk. Wait a minute – what's that in the corner? Why it's . . .

It was a warm, clear evening, perfect for sitting outside in the backyard looking at the stars. Darlene was helping Gina find the Big Dipper constellation. Suddenly there was a flash . . .

Lightning streaked across the sky! Thunder rumbled! The lights flicked off – on – off – on – off! It is so dark! Then there was a soft knock at the door and . . .

You wake up one morning and find yourself in a very strange land. Write about this imaginary place. How did you get there and what is it like to live there?

You are walking with your friends in the woods. You stop to look at an unusual toad. When you look back up, you cannot see or hear your friends. All you hear is a scratching noise in the leaves. What happens next?

Who? What? When? Where?

Name _____

a circle around the words: red—who   blue—what

yellow—when   green—where

Write the words in the correct clouds.

Who

what

today

yesterday

morning

brother   spoon   popcorn

cowboy   tonight   under the tree

teacher

upstairs   light

friends   in a bag

on the table   bottle

when

where

Movie Match

Name _____

Look at the movie screen. Read the sentences. 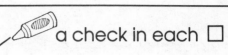 a check in each ☐ that tells what is shown in the screen.

A. ☐ The house has five rooms.
☐ The huge house sits on a hill.

B. ☐ It is a cloudy night.
☐ It is a cloudy day.

C. ☐ The robber is hiding behind the tree.
☐ The robber is sleeping under the tree.

D. ☐ The owl is flying in the sky.
☐ The owl is sitting in the tree.

E. ☐ The kids are walking up the hill.
☐ The kids are leaving the house.

F. ☐ The robber's footprints are gone.
☐ The robber's footprints are easy to see.

The Farmer and the Tiger
Use with page 31.

Name _____

Use the glossary to write the English words above each of the Chinese characters.

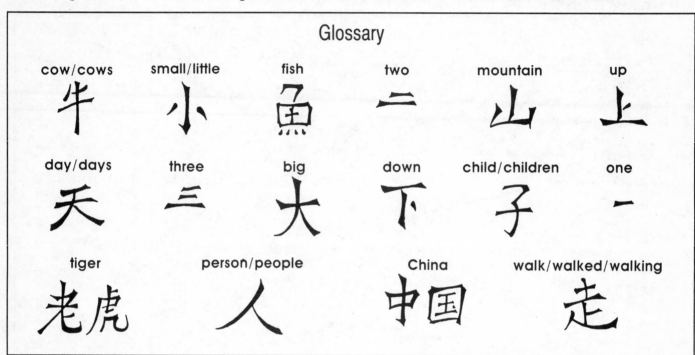

In 中国 there once lived a farmer whose 牛 no longer gave milk. Such a disaster!

Now his 三 小 子 would have no milk. And so the farmer 走

to the neighboring villages, looking for a 人 who might exchange a 牛 for labor.

He looked 上 and 下 the countryside until at last he came to a 大

山 on which a fierce 老虎 lived. Now this 老虎 was very hungry.

He crouched and hid his body, thinking he might eat the farmer for his meal.

 IF450 Substitute Survival Kit

The Farmer and the Tiger
Use with page 30.

But the farmer, whose eyes were very good, saw the swishing tail of the 老虎 .

The farmer reached into his belt, pulled out a horn, raised it to his mouth and blew as loudly

as he could. Quickly 二 人 who had been catching 魚 in a nearby

river came running. Because they were so smeared with mud they frightened the

sharp-toothed 老虎 away.

After such a great victory, the men generously offered the farmer a new 牛 .

He agreed to build the men a trap that very 天 with which to capture the 大

老虎 . And so it happened!

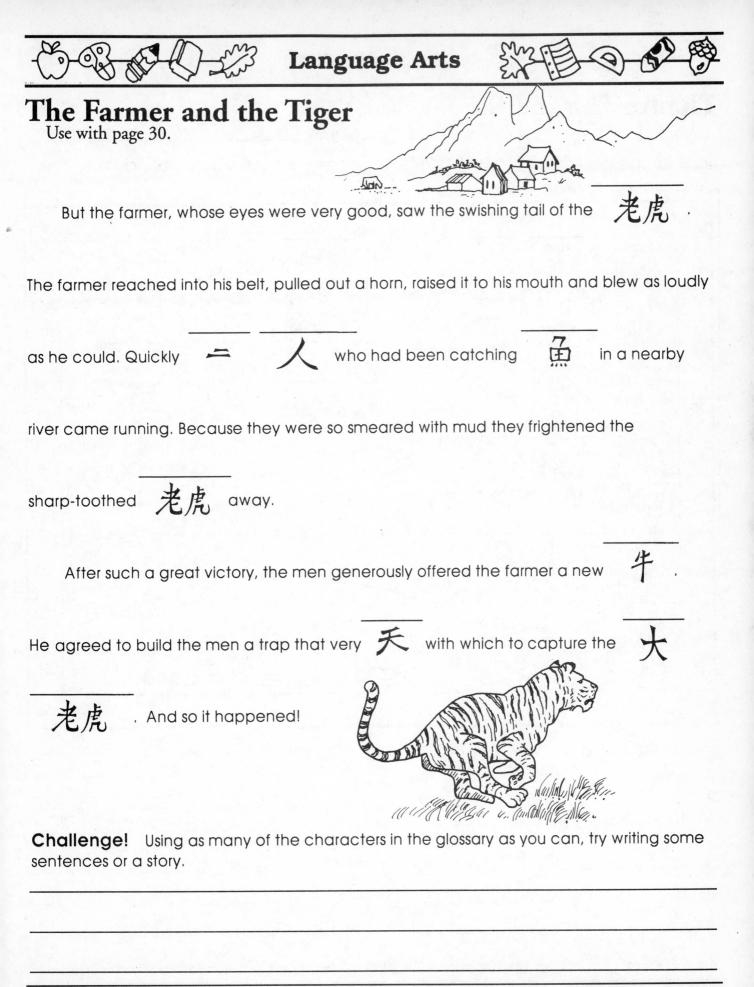

Challenge! Using as many of the characters in the glossary as you can, try writing some sentences or a story.

_____

_____

_____

Picture This

Name _____

Look at the portrait of the lady. Write 14 phrases about what the lady and her life might have been like.

1 _____
2 _____
3 _____
4 _____
5 _____
6 _____
7 _____

8 _____
9 _____
10 _____
11 _____
12 _____
13 _____
14 _____

Awesome Arabic

Name _____

Use the original Arabic word and the English definition to find each English word. **Hint:** If necessary, use a dictionary which gives roots and origins. Sources may vary on original spellings.

Challenge! See how many you can do without using a dictionary!

Original	Today's English Meaning	Word in English
suffah	a wide, upholstered seat	_ _ _ _ _
jamal	a large desert animal with a humped back	_ _ _ _ _
al birquq	a small peach-like fruit	_ _ _ _ _ _ _
qandi	a flavored syrup hardened into small pieces for eating	_ _ _ _ _
attabi	any striped or brindled cat	_ _ _ _ _
shal	a large, broad scarf	_ _ _ _ _
tarifa	taxes placed on imported goods	_ _ _ _ _ _
makhzan	a place where things are stored; a periodical filled with articles	_ _ _ _ _ _ _ _
al-manakh	a yearly calendar which forecasts weather and lists many facts	_ _ _ _ _ _ _
laymun	a sour, light-yellow fruit	_ _ _ _ _
qutn	soft, white plant fibers used to make cloth	_ _ _ _ _ _
al-jabr	type of mathematics which uses letters	_ _ _ _ _ _ _
matrah	a casing of cloth which is filled with soft material and slept upon	_ _ _ _ _ _
sukkar	a sweet substance made from the cane of a plant	_ _ _ _ _

Shop 'til You Drop

Name _____

You and your dad are going to a shopping mall today.

This is a list of the things you need to buy:

1. film for the camera _____

2. jelly beans for Grandpa _____

3. a new shirt for Dad _____

4. a gardening book for Mom _____

5. a toy for Jed's birthday _____

Look at the map of the mall. Write the store names on the lines above to show where you must go to buy what you need.

Use a blue crayon to trace a line to each of the stores in the order you listed them.

The Deli	Men's Clothing	The Card Shop	Office Needs	The Video Store	Books Galore
	MALL				Waxy Things
Fun Toys	Camera and Photo Shop	Sport Shop	(Enter Here)	Petunia's Pets	Murphy's Candy Delights

Rewrite the list of stores you need to go to so you go through the mall in the order the stores are placed. Start with **Murphy's Candy Delights.**

1. _____

2. _____

3. _____

4. _____

5. _____

TGIF

Name _____

Number the school subjects in the order that they happen during the day.
Reading is first.

____ Math — 12:00 P.M.

____ English — 10:15 A.M.

____ Social Studies — 1:30 P.M.

____ Reading — 8:00 A.M.

____ Science — 1:00 P.M.

____ Music — 10:45 A.M.

____ Library — 2:00 P.M.

____ Gym — 12:30 P.M.

____ Spelling — 9:30 A.M.

Make a time line to show the order of the subjects. Write the time in the top box. Write the subject in the bottom box. The first one is done for you.

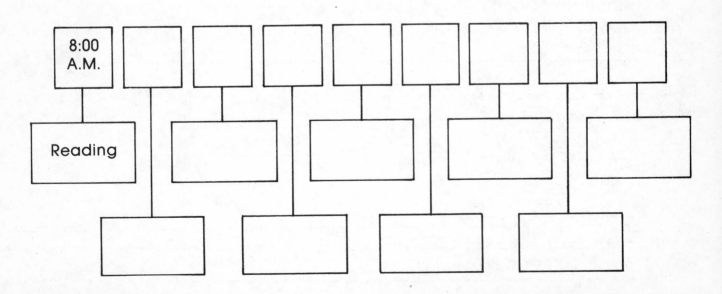

8:00 A.M.

Reading

Follow the Leader

Name _____

Place a dot in the middle of the fourth triangle.
Mark an X on the third triangle from the right.
Draw a line through the ninth triangle.
Circle the seventh triangle.

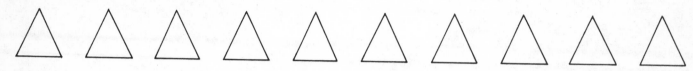

Bryon is taller than Robbie. Angela is shorter than Bryon. Robbie is fatter than Todd. Cindy is the tallest girl.
Write each person's name on the line under his or her picture.

_____ _____ _____ _____ _____

Rover has long, floppy ears and is larger than Bouncer. All the dogs have tails except Rover and Poochie. Bandit has the fattest tail. Spot has big spots. Bandit and Spotty are about the same size.
Write each dog's name on the line under its picture.

_____ _____ _____ _____ _____ _____

• Write what comes next.

A = 1, B = 3, C = 5, _____

Bird's-Eye View

Name _____

Draw the lines as directed from point to point for each graph.

Draw a line from:
F,7 to D,1
D,1 to I,6
I,6 to N,8
N,8 to M,3
M,3 to F,1
F,1 to G,4
G,4 to E,4
E,4 to B,1
B,1 to A,8
A,8 to D,11
D,11 to F,9
F,9 to F,7
F,7 to I,9
I,9 to I,6
I,6 to F,7

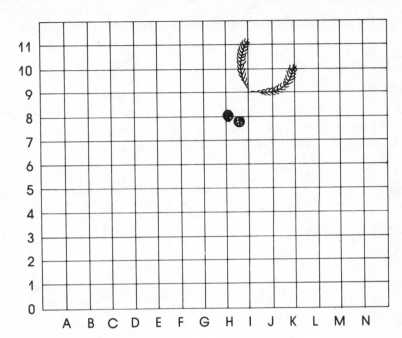

Draw a line from:
J,⊙ to N,☾
N,☾ to U,☾
U,☾ to Z,■
Z,■ to X,♡
X,♡ to U,☾
U,☾ to S,☆
S,☆ to N,☾
N,☾ to N,☆
N,☆ to J,⊙
J,⊙ to L,•
L,• to Y•
Y,• to Z,■
Z,■ to L,■
L,■ to J,⊙

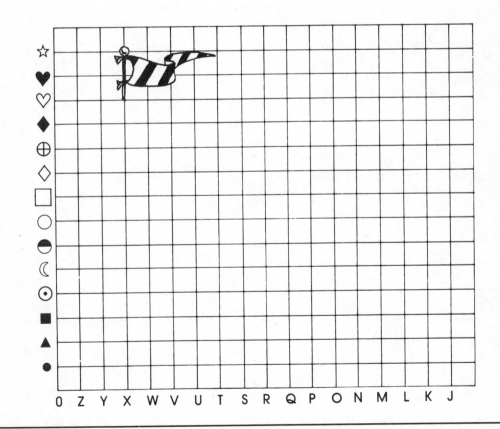

• Write what comes next.

SAD   SBF   SCH   SDJ   SEL   _____

IF450 Substitute Survival Kit

Playing the Part

Name _____

Pretend you are starring in a play about nursery rhymes. The director has given you a list of props for each nursery rhyme.

Match each prop to the correct nursery rhyme title by writing the number of the prop in the star.

Props:

1. bone	4. flowers	7. mittens	10. pumpkin
2. candlestick	5. horn	8. pail	11. shoe
3. fiddle	6. lamb	9. pipe	12. wall

What do you notice about list of props?

Weather Watching

Name _____

Weather describes the condition of the air for a period of time. Weather maps contain symbols that describe the weather.

Below is a calendar for an imaginary month. Beside it is a key for some weather symbols. Fill in the squares for each day of the month with the correct weather symbols by following the directions carefully.

Key

rain

snow

clouds

fog

sun

hail

sleet

Sun.	Mon.	Tues.	Wed.	Thurs.	Fri.	Sat.
	1	2	3	4	5	6
7	8	9	10	11	12	13
14	15	16	17	18	19	20
21	22	23	24	25	26	27
28	29	30	31			

Directions

1. All days whose sum of digits equals 8 are foggy.
2. Two diagonally adjoining even-numbered days whose sum equals 36 are snowy.
3. Odd-numbered days that follow a foggy day are rainy.
4. All Saturdays except one are sunny.
5. The first, middle, and last days of the month have weather that begins with an **s** and hasn't been mentioned yet.
6. Cloudy days precede all foggy days except one.
7. Cloudy days follow all snowy days.
8. Only two Thursdays are cloudy, and they are two weeks apart.
9. Two Sundays of the month have hail.
10. The rest of the even-numbered days are the same as the majority of Saturdays.
11. The remaining days are cloudy.

A Slow Stroll

Name _____

Connect the dots in alphabetical order.
Start with the word **across**.
Color the picture.

let's

main •

• rain

• across

• keep

• note   wagon •   • soft

quick •

very   • before •

• zoo   • x-ray

• your   • teeth

• penny   • use

cold •

older •

• hole   • joke

ill

• food   •

• don't

garden

easy

Word Puzzles

Safari Crossing

Name _____

Read the clues. Write the matching words found in the maze.

1. Blouses _____
2. Baby dogs _____
3. Small make-believe people
   _____
4. The United States, Mexico and Canada are. . . _____
5. Large towns _____
6. White flowers _____
7. Celebrations_____
8. Very young children _____
9. Women _____

10. Tales _____
11. Cents _____
12. Small horses_____
13. Small round treats _____
14. Moms, dads and children make. . . _____
15. Flying insects _____
16. Young rabbits _____
17. Red fruit that grows on trees
    _____
18. Places where goods are made _____

Trace a path along the rocks in the order of your answers. You will reach the other side of the river.

cities lilies
countries parties babies
elves
armies ladies
stories
puppies pennies
shirts
ponies
groceries
quarries cookies
studies
flies families
bunnies cherries factories

A (Pot-Top)

Name _____

An **anagram** is a word made by rearranging the letters of another word. Find at least two anagrams for each word below and write your answers on the spaces.

Example: taps – pats, spat

1. hears _____
2. peal _____
3. elbow _____
4. adder _____
5. stain _____
6. vile _____
7. inks _____
8. heaps _____
9. tester _____
10. parts _____
11. onset _____
12. tares _____
13. sepal _____
14. veers _____
15. layer _____
16. mean _____
17. heals _____
18. raspy _____
19. huts _____

Substitute Survival Kit

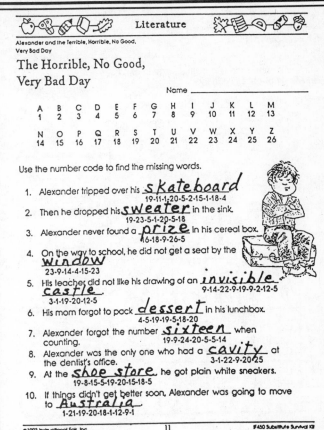

Literature

Alexander and the Terrible, Horrible, No Good,
Very Bad Day

The Horrible, No Good,
Very Bad Day

Name _____

| A 1 | B 2 | C 3 | D 4 | E 5 | F 6 | G 7 | H 8 | I 9 | J 10 | K 11 | L 12 | M 13 |
| N 14 | O 15 | P 16 | Q 17 | R 18 | S 19 | T 20 | U 21 | V 22 | W 23 | X 24 | Y 25 | Z 26 |

Use the number code to find the missing words.

1. Alexander tripped over his _skateboard_
   19-11-1-20-5-2-15-1-18-4
2. Then he dropped his _sweater_ in the sink.
   19-23-5-1-20-5-18
3. Alexander never found a _prize_ in his cereal box.
   16-18-9-26-5
4. On the way to school, he did not get a seat by the
   window
   23-9-14-4-15-23
5. His teacher did not like his drawing of an _invisible_
   castle.   9-14-22-9-19-9-2-12-5
   3-1-19-20-12-5
6. His mom forgot to pack _dessert_ in his lunchbox.
   4-5-19-19-5-18-20
7. Alexander forgot the number _sixteen_ when
   counting.   19-9-24-20-5-5-14
8. Alexander was the only one who had a _cavity_ at
   the dentist's office.   3-1-22-9-20-25
9. At the _shoe store_ he got plain white sneakers.
   19-8-15-5-19-20-15-18-5
10. If things didn't get better soon, Alexander was going to move
    to _Australia_
    1-21-19-20-18-1-12-9-1

©1993 Instructional Fair, Inc.   11   IF450 Substitute Survival Kit

---

Literature

Miss Nelson Is Missing!/Miss Nelson Is Back

Desk Jockeys

Name _____

Put the words from Miss Nelson's desk under the characters they best describe.
Then draw the characters in the boxes below the word lists.

Miss Nelson	Mr. Blandsworth	Viola Swamp
blonde	boring	black finger-
ill	man	strict nails
soft-spoken	confused	substitute
sweet	principal	loud
kind	mustache	mean
sore throat	funny tie	black dress

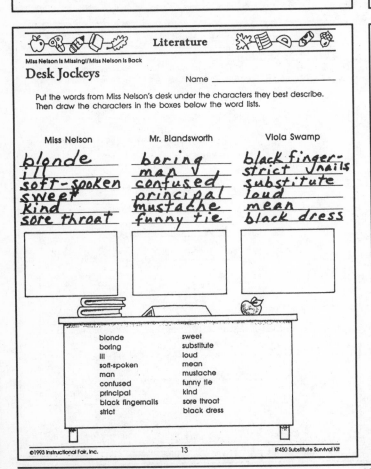

blonde · sweet
boring · substitute
ill · loud
soft-spoken · mean
man · mustache
confused · funny tie
principal · kind
black fingernails · sore throat
strict · black dress

©1993 Instructional Fair, Inc.   13   IF450 Substitute Survival Kit

---

Math

Farm Shapes

Name _____

Color: brown yellow green red

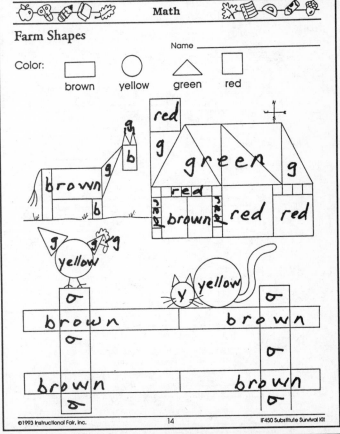

©1993 Instructional Fair, Inc.   14   IF450 Substitute Survival Kit

---

Math

Subtraction Hill

Name _____

Work all problems to find path. Shade in all answers that have a 3 in them.

	$\begin{array}{r}98\\-52\\\hline 46\end{array}$	$\begin{array}{r}46\\-12\\\hline 34\end{array}$	$\begin{array}{r}68\\-17\\\hline 51\end{array}$
$\begin{array}{r}79\\-53\\\hline 26\end{array}$	$\begin{array}{r}65\\-23\\\hline 42\end{array}$	$\begin{array}{r}63\\-31\\\hline 32\end{array}$	$\begin{array}{r}86\\-32\\\hline 54\end{array}$
$\begin{array}{r}59\\-45\\\hline 14\end{array}$	$\begin{array}{r}75\\-64\\\hline 11\end{array}$	$\begin{array}{r}67\\-24\\\hline 43\end{array}$	$\begin{array}{r}97\\-54\\\hline 43\end{array}$	$\begin{array}{r}55\\-43\\\hline 12\end{array}$
$\begin{array}{r}87\\-65\\\hline 22\end{array}$	$\begin{array}{r}44\\-32\\\hline 12\end{array}$	$\begin{array}{r}57\\-24\\\hline 33\end{array}$	$\begin{array}{r}88\\-25\\\hline 63\end{array}$	$\begin{array}{r}75\\-61\\\hline 14\end{array}$	$\begin{array}{r}48\\-26\\\hline 22\end{array}$
$\begin{array}{r}69\\-25\\\hline 44\end{array}$	$\begin{array}{r}95\\-24\\\hline 71\end{array}$	$\begin{array}{r}48\\-13\\\hline 35\end{array}$	$\begin{array}{r}58\\-16\\\hline 42\end{array}$	$\begin{array}{r}35\\-13\\\hline 22\end{array}$	$\begin{array}{r}39\\-17\\\hline 22\end{array}$

©1993 Instructional Fair, Inc.   15   IF450 Substitute Survival Kit

---

Math

Shape Mates

Match the congruent figures.

Name _____

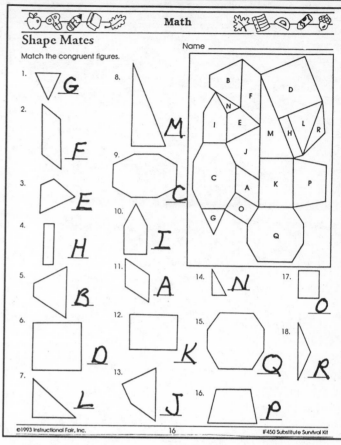

1. G
2. F
3. E
4. H
5. B
6. D
7. L
8. M
9. C
10. I
11. A
12. K
13. J
14. N
15. Q
16. P
17. O
18. R

©1993 Instructional Fair, Inc.   16   IF450 Substitute Survival Kit

---

Math

Minute Maid

Name _____

How long does it take the "Minute Maid" to do her household tasks?

	Time Started	Length of Task	Time Ended
Polishing	Example 9:14	35 minutes	9:49
Dusting	7:18	42 minutes	8:00
Waxing	10:03	48 min.	10:51
Mopping	2:36	29 minutes	3:05
Cleaning Windows	4:45	47 min.	5:32
Serving Breakfast	7:12	18 minutes	7:30
Laundry	11:10	58 minutes	12:08
Ironing	12:13	47 min.	1:00
Serving Lunch	11:30	24 minutes	11:54
Vacuuming	3:16	41 minutes	3:57
Serving Dinner	5:30	27 min.	5:57
Hanging Curtains	6:26	56 minutes	7:22
Making Beds	8:03	38 min.	8:41

©1993 Instructional Fair, Inc.   17   IF450 Substitute Survival Kit

---

Math

One-Stop Shopping

Name _____

Stash McCash is shopping! Find the total cost of the items. Then find how much change Stash should receive.

$3.36 Stickers $.94 $.27 $2.68 $4.25
$1.54 $3.15 $1.49
$3.99 $.88 $2.49 $2.55
$3.61 $.77 $1.27

Example

Stash has $5.00 Buys	Stash has $8.50 Buys	Stash has $7.04 Buys	Stash has $9.00 Buys
.88 .77 +1.54 3.19	$1.27 3.99 2.68 $7.94	$1.49 3.15 .27 $4.91	$3.15 3.61 .88 $7.64
5.00 −3.19 1.81 Change	8.50 −7.94 .56 $.56 Change	7.04 −4.91 $2.13 Change	9.00 −7.64 1.36 Change

Stash has $10.95 Buys	Stash has $10.00 Buys	Stash has $9.24 Buys	Stash has $8.09 Buys
$3.36 2.49 4.25 $10.10	$2.55 3.61 .94 $7.10	$4.25 1.27 1.54 $7.06	$2.49 2.68 .94 $6.11
10.95 −10.10 $.85 Change	10.00 −7.10 $2.90 Change	9.24 −7.06 $2.18 Change	8.09 −6.11 $1.98 Change

©1993 Instructional Fair, Inc.   18   IF450 Substitute Survival Kit

---

Math

Step Right Up

Name _____

Start at the bottom of the steps. Write your answer at the top.

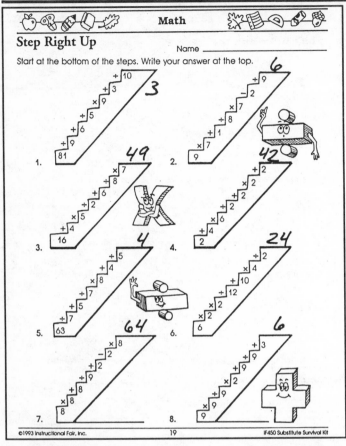

1. 49
2. 42
3. 4
4. 24
5. 64
6. 6
7.
8.

Social Studies

Map It Out

Name _____

Use the legend box to answer the questions.

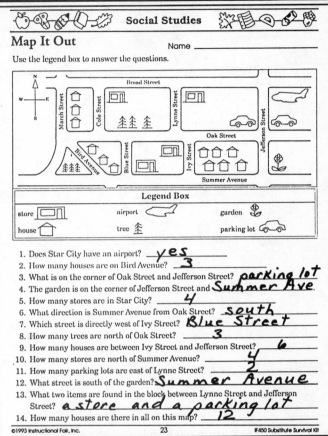

Legend Box

store — house — airport — tree — garden — parking lot

1. Does Star City have an airport? __yes__
2. How many houses are on Bird Avenue? __3__
3. What is on the corner of Oak Street and Jefferson Street? __parking lot__
4. The garden is on the corner of Jefferson Street and __Summer Ave.__
5. How many stores are in Star City? __4__
6. What direction is Summer Avenue from Oak Street? __south__
7. Which street is directly west of Ivy Street? __Blue Street__
8. How many trees are north of Oak Street? __3__
9. How many houses are between Ivy Street and Jefferson Street? __6__
10. How many stores are north of Summer Avenue? __4__
11. How many parking lots are east of Lynne Street? __2__
12. What street is south of the garden? __Summer Avenue__
13. What two items are found in the block between Lynne Street and Jefferson Street? __a store and a parking lot__
14. How many houses are there in all on this map? __12__

Language Arts

Who? What? When? Where?

Name _____

Draw a circle around the words: red—who   blue—what
yellow—when   green—where

Write the words in the correct clouds.

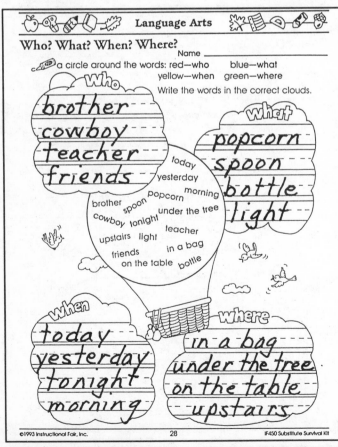

Who: brother, cowboy, teacher, friends

What: popcorn, spoon, bottle, light

When: today, yesterday, tonight, morning

Where: in a bag, under the tree, on the table, upstairs

(word bank: today, yesterday, morning, brother, spoon, popcorn, cowboy, tonight, under the tree, teacher, upstairs, light, in a bag, friends, on the table, bottle)

Language Arts

Movie Match

Name _____

Look at the movie screen. Read the sentences. Place a check in each ☐ that tells what is shown in the screen.

A. ☐ The house has five rooms.
   ☒ The huge house sits on a hill.

B. ☒ It is a cloudy night.
   ☐ It is a cloudy day.

C. ☒ The robber is hiding behind the tree.
   ☐ The robber is sleeping under the tree.

D. ☐ The owl is flying in the sky.
   ☒ The owl is sitting in the tree.

E. ☒ The kids are walking up the hill.
   ☐ The kids are leaving the house.

F. ☐ The robber's footprints are gone.
   ☒ The robber's footprints are easy to see.

Answer Key

Language Arts

The Farmer and the Tiger
Use with page 31.   Name _____

Use the glossary to write the English words above each of the Chinese characters.

Glossary					
cow/cows	small/little	fish	two	mountain	up
牛	小	魚	二	山	上
day/days	three	big	down	child/children	one
天	三	大	下	子	一
tiger	person/people		China	walk/walked/walking	
老虎	人		中国	走	

China

In 中国 there once lived a farmer whose 牛 **cow(s)** no longer gave milk. Such a disaster!

Now his 三 **three** 小 **small** 子 **children** would have no milk. And so the farmer 走 **walked**

to the neighboring villages, looking for a 人 **person** who might exchange a 牛 **cow** for labor.

He looked 上 **up** and 下 **down** the countryside until at last he came to a **big**

mountain 山 on which a fierce 老虎 **tiger** lived. Now this 老虎 **tiger** was very hungry.

He crouched 下 **down** and hid his body, thinking he might eat the farmer for his meal.

©1993 Instructional Fair, Inc.   30   IF450 Substitute Survival Kit

---

Language Arts

The Farmer and the Tiger
Use with page 30.

But the farmer, whose eyes were very good, saw the swishing tail of the **tiger** 老虎

The farmer reached into his belt, pulled out a horn, raised it to his mouth and blew as loudly

as he could. Quickly 二 **two** 人 **people** who had been catching 魚 **fish** in a nearby

river came running. Because they were so smeared with mud they frightened the

sharp-toothed 老虎 **tiger** away.

After such a great victory, the men generously offered the farmer a new **cow** 牛

He agreed to build the men a trap that very 天 **day** with which to capture the **big** 大

tiger 老虎 . And so it happened!

Challenge! Using as many of the characters in the glossary as you can, try writing some sentences or a story.

_____

_____

©1993 Instructional Fair, Inc.   31   IF450 Substitute Survival Kit

---

Language Arts

Awesome Arabic
                     Name _____

Use the original Arabic word and the English definition to find each English word. Hint: If necessary, use a dictionary which gives roots and origins. Sources may vary on original spellings.

Challenge! See how many you can do without using a dictionary!

Original	Today's English Meaning	Word in English
suffah	a wide, upholstered seat	sofa
jamal	a large desert animal with a humped back	camel
al birquq	a small peach-like fruit	apricot
qandi	a flavored syrup hardened into small pieces for eating	candy
attabi	any striped or brindled cat	tabby
shal	a large, broad scarf	shawl
tarifa	taxes placed on imported goods	tariff
makhzan	a place where things are stored; a periodical filled with articles	magazine
al-manakh	a yearly calendar which forecasts weather and lists many facts	almanac
laymun	a sour, light-yellow fruit	lemon
qutn	soft, white plant fibers used to make cloth	cotton
al-jabr	type of mathematics which uses letters	algebra
matrah	a casing of cloth which is filled with soft material and slept upon	mattress
sukkar	a sweet substance made from the cane of a plant	sugar

©1993 Instructional Fair, Inc.   33   IF450 Substitute Survival Kit

---

Sequencing

Shop 'til You Drop
                     Name _____

You and your dad are going to a shopping mall today.

This is a list of the things you need to buy:
1. film for the camera — **Camera and Photo Shop**
2. jelly beans for Grandpa — **Murphy's Candy Delights**
3. a new shirt for Dad — **Men's Clothing**
4. a gardening book for Mom — **Books Galore**
5. a toy for Jed's birthday — **Fun Toys**

Look at the map of the mall. Write the store names on the lines above to show where you must go to buy what you need.

Use a blue crayon to trace a line to each of the stores in the order you listed them.

The Deli	Men's Clothing	The Card Shop	Office Needs	The Video Store	Books Galore
			MALL		Waxy Things
Fun Toys	Camera and Photo Shop	Sport Shop	(Enter Here)	Petunia's Pets	Murphy's Candy Delights

Rewrite the list of stores you need to go to so you go through the mall in the order the stores are placed. Start with Murphy's Candy Delights.
1. Murphy's Candy Delights
2. Books Galore
3. Men's Clothing
4. Fun Toys
5. Camera and Photo Shop

©1993 Instructional Fair, Inc.   34   IF450 Substitute Survival Kit

---

©1993 Instructional Fair, Inc.   46   IF450 Substitute Survival Kit

Answer Key

Sequencing

TGIF

Name _____

Number the school subjects in the order that they happen during the day.
Reading is first.

5 Math — 12:00 P.M.
3 English — 10:15 A.M.
8 Social Studies — 1:30 P.M.
1 Reading — 8:00 A.M.
7 Science — 1:00 P.M.
4 Music — 10:45 A.M.
9 Library — 2:00 P.M.
6 Gym — 12:30 P.M.
2 Spelling — 9:30 A.M.

Make a time line to show the order of the subjects. Write the time in the top box. Write the subject in the bottom box. The first one is done for you.

8:00 A.M.	9:30 A.M.	10:15 A.M.	10:45 A.M.	12:00 P.M.	12:30 P.M.	1:00 P.M.	1:30 P.M.	2:00 P.M.
Reading		English	Math		Science			Library
	Spelling	Music		Gym			Social Studies	

©1993 Instructional Fair, Inc. — 35 — IF450 Substitute Survival Kit

Sequencing

Follow the Leader

Name _____

Place a dot in the middle of the fourth triangle.
Mark an X on the third triangle from the right.
Draw a line through the ninth triangle.
Circle the seventh triangle.

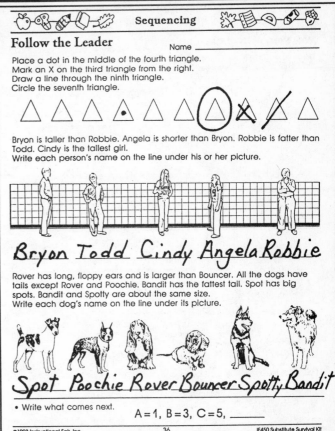

Bryon is taller than Robbie. Angela is shorter than Bryon. Robbie is fatter than Todd. Cindy is the tallest girl.
Write each person's name on the line under his or her picture.

Bryon Todd Cindy Angela Robbie

Rover has long, floppy ears and is larger than Bouncer. All the dogs have tails except Rover and Poochie. Bandit has the fattest tail. Spot has big spots. Bandit and Spotty are about the same size.
Write each dog's name on the line under its picture.

Spot Poochie Rover Bouncer Spotty Bandit

• Write what comes next.   A = 1, B = 3, C = 5, ___

©1993 Instructional Fair, Inc. — 36 — IF450 Substitute Survival Kit

Sequencing

Bird's-Eye View

Name _____

Draw the lines as directed from point to point for each graph.

Draw a line from:
F,7 to D,1
D,1 to I,6
I,6 to N,8
N,8 to M,3
M,3 to F,1
F,1 to G,4
G,4 to E,4
E,4 to B,1
B,1 to A,8
A,8 to D,11
D,11 to F,9
F,9 to F,7
F,7 to I,9
I,9 to I,6
I,6 to F,7

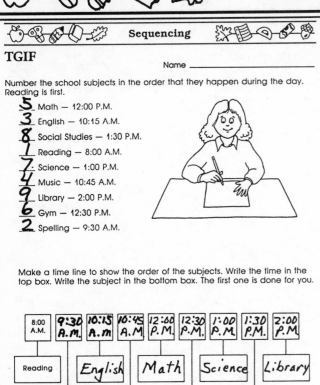

Draw a line from:
J,⊙ to N,☾
N,☾ to U,☾
U,☾ to Z,■
Z,■ to X,♡
X,♡ to U,☾
U,☾ to S,☆
S,☆ to N,☾
N,☾ to N,☆
N,☆ to J,⊙
J,⊙ to L,•
L,• to Y,•
Y,• to Z,■
Z,■ to L,■
L,■ to J,⊙

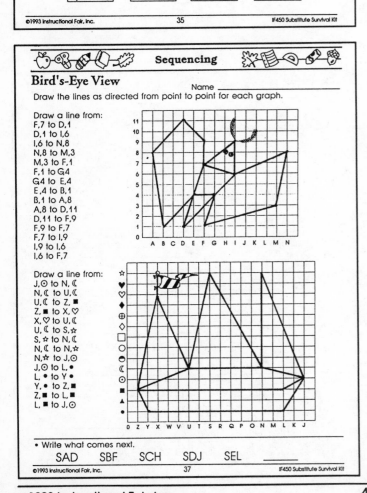

• Write what comes next.
SAD   SBF   SCH   SDJ   SEL   ___

©1993 Instructional Fair, Inc. — 37 — IF450 Substitute Survival Kit

Critical Thinking

Playing the Part

Name _____

Pretend you are starring in a play about nursery rhymes. The director has given you a list of props for each nursery rhyme.

Match each prop to the correct nursery rhyme title by writing the number of the prop in the star.

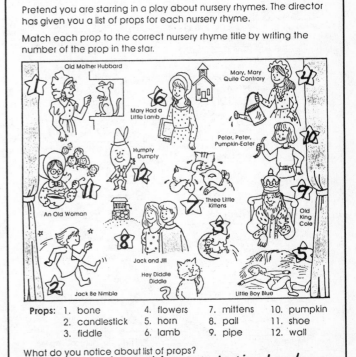

Props:
1. bone
2. candlestick
3. fiddle
4. flowers
5. horn
6. lamb
7. mittens
8. pail
9. pipe
10. pumpkin
11. shoe
12. wall

What do you notice about list of props?
They are listed in alphabetical order.

©1993 Instructional Fair, Inc. — 38 — IF450 Substitute Survival Kit

©1993 Instructional Fair, Inc.   47   IF450 Substitute Survival Kit

Weather Watching

Name _____

Weather describes the condition of the air for a period of time. Weather maps contain symbols that describe the weather.

Below is a calendar for an imaginary month. Beside it is a key for some weather symbols. Fill in the squares for each day of the month with the correct weather symbols by following the directions carefully.

Key

rain
snow
clouds
fog
sun
hail
sleet

	Sun.	Mon.	Tues.	Wed.	Thurs.	Fri.	Sat.
			2	3	4	5	6
	7	8	9	10	11	12	13
	14	15	16	17	18	19	20
	21	22	23	24	25	26	27
	28	29	30	31			

Directions

1. All days whose sum of digits equals 8 are foggy.
2. Two diagonally adjoining even-numbered days whose sum equals 36 are snowy.
3. Odd-numbered days that follow a foggy day are rainy.
4. All Saturdays except one are sunny.
5. The first, middle, and last days of the month have weather that begins with an s and hasn't been mentioned yet.
6. Cloudy days precede all foggy days except one.
7. Cloudy days follow all snowy days.
8. Only two Thursdays are cloudy, and they are two weeks apart.
9. Two Sundays of the month have hail.
10. The rest of the even-numbered days are the same as the majority of Saturdays.
11. The remaining days are cloudy.

©1993 Instructional Fair, Inc.   39   IF450 Substitute Survival Kit

---

A Slow Stroll

Name _____

Connect the dots in alphabetical order.
Start with the word across.
Color the picture.

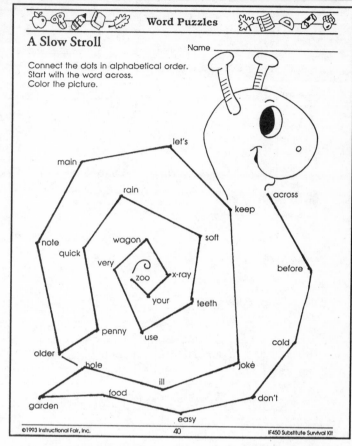

let's
main
across
rain
keep
note
wagon
soft
quick
very
before
zoo
x-ray
your
teeth
penny
use
older
cold
hole
joke
ill
food
don't
garden
easy

©1993 Instructional Fair, Inc.   40   IF450 Substitute Survival Kit

---

Safari Crossing

Name _____

Read the clues. Write the matching words found in the maze.

1. Blouses **shirts**
2. Baby dogs **puppies**
3. Small make-believe people **elves**
4. The United States, Mexico and Canada are... **countries**
5. Large towns **cities**
6. White flowers **lilies**
7. Celebrations **parties**
8. Very young children **babies**
9. Women **ladies**
10. Tales **stories**
11. Cents **pennies**
12. Small horses **ponies**
13. Small round treats **cookies**
14. Moms, dads and children make... **families**
15. Flying insects **flies**
16. Young rabbits **bunnies**
17. Red fruit that grows on trees **cherries**
18. Places where goods are made **factories**

Trace a path along the rocks in the order of your answers. You will reach the other side of the river.

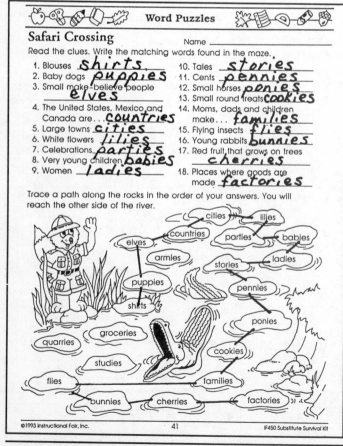

©1993 Instructional Fair, Inc.   41   IF450 Substitute Survival Kit

---

A (Pot-Top)

Name _____

An anagram is a word made by rearranging the letters of another word. Find at least two anagrams for each word below and write your answers on the spaces.

Example: taps – pats, spat

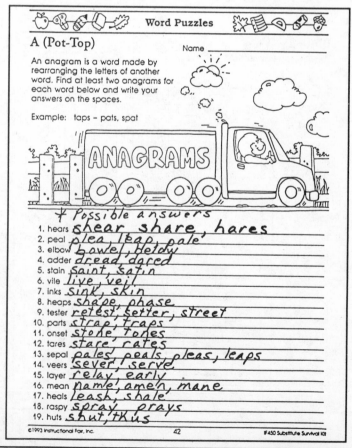

* Possible answers

1. hears **shear, share, hares**
2. peal **plea, leap, pale**
3. elbow **bowel, below**
4. adder **dread, dared**
5. stain **saint, satin**
6. vile **live, veil**
7. inks **sink, skin**
8. heaps **shape, phase**
9. tester **retest, setter, street**
10. parts **strap, traps**
11. onset **stone, tones**
12. tares **stare, rates**
13. sepal **pales, peals, pleas, leaps**
14. veers **sever, serve**
15. layer **relay, early**
16. mean **name, amen, mane**
17. heals **leash, shale**
18. raspy **spray, prays**
19. huts **shut, thus**

©1993 Instructional Fair, Inc.   42   IF450 Substitute Survival Kit

---

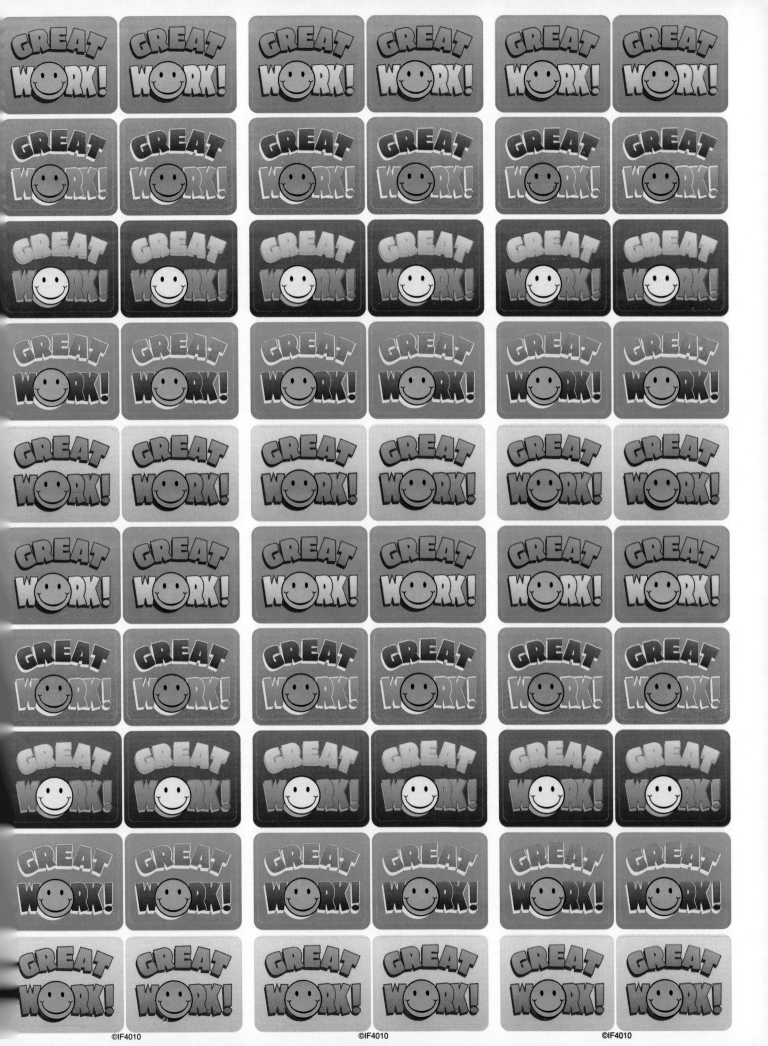

©IF4010

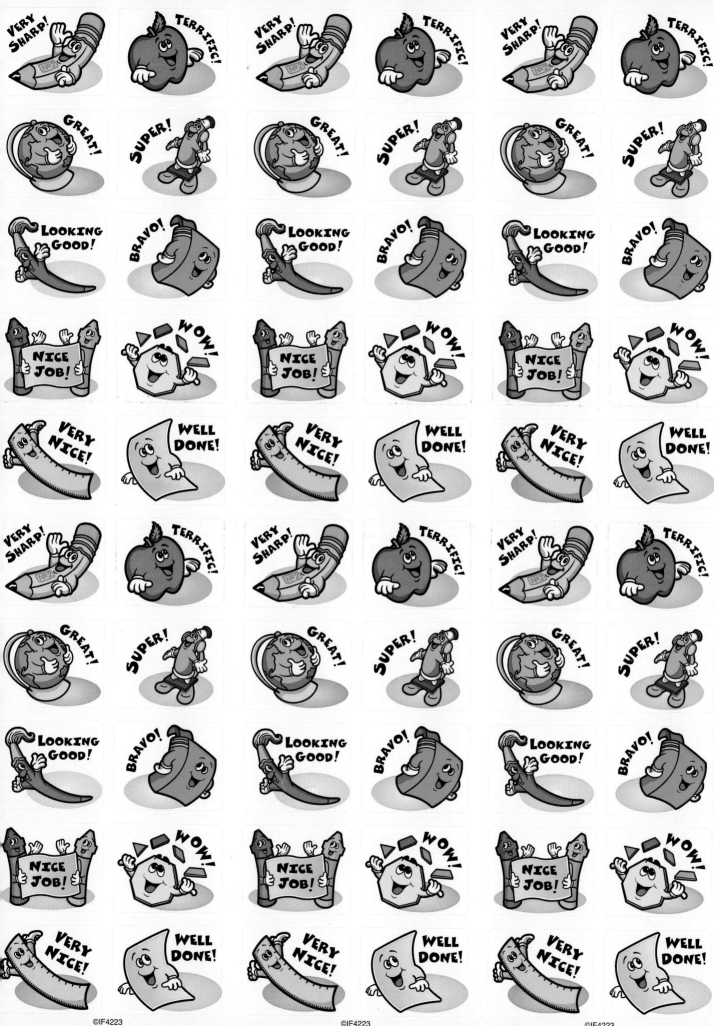

©IF4223

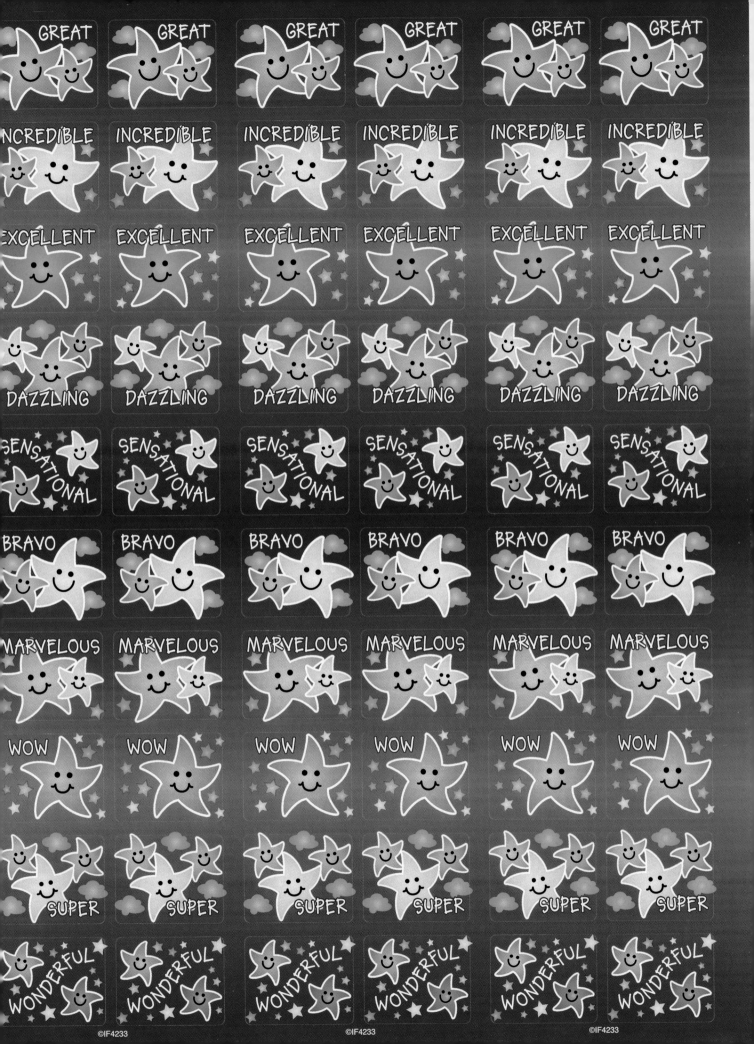